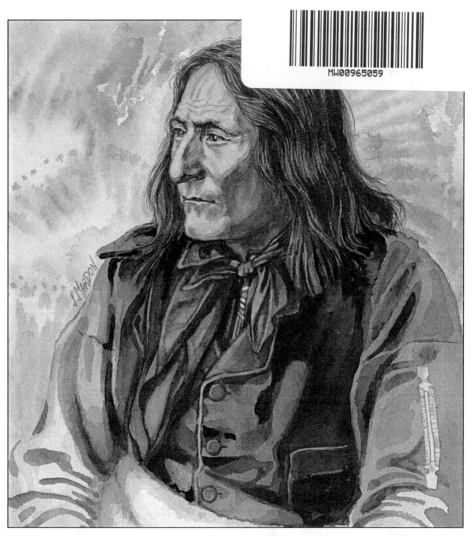

Crowfoot

Carlotta Hacker

Fitzhenry & Whiteside Limited

Contents

THE CANADIANS
A Continuing Series

Crowfoot

Author: Carlotta Hacker
Design: Kerry Designs
Cover Illustration: John Mardon

Canadian Cataloguing in Publication Data
Hacker, Carlotta, 1931-
Crowfoot
(The Canadians)
Bibliography: P. 64
ISBN 1-55041-467-4
1. Crowfoot, Blackfoot chief, 1830-1890 2. Indians of North America – Prairie Provinces – Biography.
3. Indians of North America – Prairie Provinces – Government relations. I. Title. II. Series
E99.S54C76   970.004'97   C99-10321-1

© 1999 Fitzhenry & Whiteside Limited
195 Allstate Parkway, Markham, Ontario L3R 4T8

Chapter 1

Son of a Great Nation

In 1835, a five-year-old boy set out alone to find his mother. His name was Astoxkomi (Shot Close), and he belonged to the Blood First Nation which lived in the open prairies and woodlands of the region that is now southern Alberta. His father, Istowun-eh'pata, had been killed on a raid a couple of years earlier, and his mother, Axkyahp-say-pi, had recently taken a new husband. She had married a man from the Blackfoot First Nation.

Astoxkomi had watched as his mother packed her belongings onto a travois, said farewell to her relatives, and rode away with the Blackfoot warrior. She had taken

Blackfoot woman with travois

Astoxkomi's baby brother with her but decided that Astoxkomi himself would remain behind to be brought up by his grandfather. Grandson and grandfather were such close friends that she did not like to separate them.

It was true that Astoxkomi adored his grandfather, but Axkyahp-say-pi had not reckoned with the boy's love for her. Slipping quietly out of camp, he picked up his mother's trail and set off after her. He was on foot, while she was on horseback, but she was travelling slowly because of the travois. If he ran fast enough, there was a chance he would catch up.

The child may or may not have been aware of the dangers he faced in setting out alone and unprotected. He could have been attacked by one of the many grizzly bears which roamed the countryside in those days. He could have stumbled onto an enemy patrol. He could have lost his way. But he never in his life lacked either determination or bravery. On he ran, following the trail that had been left by the marks of the travois. Hours later, way out on the open prairie, his mother saw the small figure running towards her. She had no choice but to turn back. The boy would have been missed and his relatives would be searching anxiously for him. So back they all went. Some time later, when the newlyweds once again set out from the Blood camp, Astoxkomi and his grandfather were travelling with them.

This is one of many famous stories about the boy who was first called Astoxkomi, then took the Blackfoot name of Kyiah-sta-ah (Bear Ghost), and later took his dead father's name of Istowun-eh'pata (Packs a Knife). A male Aboriginal some-times had as many as eight or nine different names during his life. Each name replaced the previous one as he grew to man-hood or performed a special act of bravery. Astoxkomi was a teenager when he earned the name that he was to make famous throughout Canada and the world: Isapo-muxika (Crow Indian's Big Foot). He kept this name for the rest of his life; it was shortened to Crowfoot by interpreters.

Because of his determination at the age of five, Crowfoot was brought up within the Blackfoot Nation instead of the Blood Nation. This was not quite like changing his nationality. The Blood, Blackfoot and Piegan all spoke the same Algonkian language and were all part of one large nation, called the Nitsitapi (Real People) which was known to

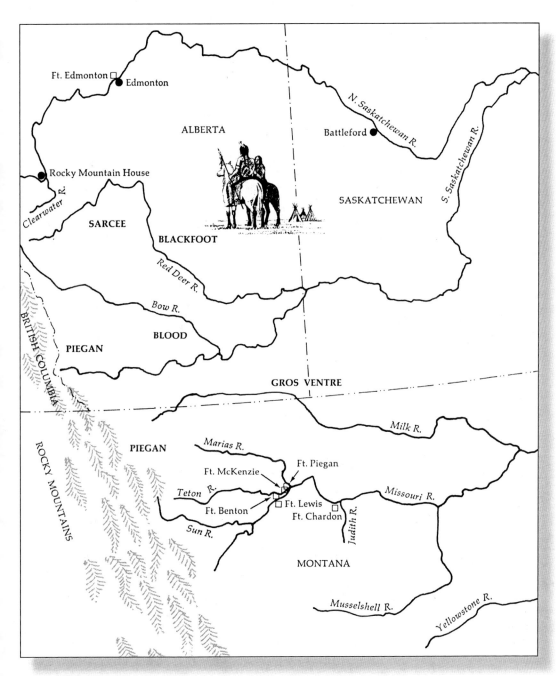

ALBERTA

Ft. Edmonton □ ● Edmonton

N. Saskatchewan R.

Battleford ●

● Rocky Mountain House

Clearwater R.

SASKATCHEWAN

S. Saskatchewan R.

SARCEE

BLACKFOOT

Red Deer R.

Bow R.

BLOOD

PIEGAN

GROS VENTRE

BRITISH COLUMBIA

Milk R.

PIEGAN

Marias R.

Ft. McKenzie

Ft. Piegan

Teton R.

□ Ft. Lewis

Ft. Benton

□ Ft. Chardon

Missouri R.

Judith R.

Sun R.

ROCKY MOUNTAINS

MONTANA

Musselshell R.

Yellowstone R.

Location of the Blackfoot Confederacy First Nations and the fur trading posts in Crowfoot's youth

A buffalo hunt

There was a shortage of horses in the north, and at times the Blackfoot even sold horses to the Hudson's Bay Company posts there.

outsiders as the Blackfoot Confederacy. The Sarcee and Gros Ventre were allies in the Confederacy although they did not speak Algonkian. The Crow, Cree, Stoney and all other neighbouring First Nations were enemies.

The members of the Blackfoot Confederacy were in a very strong position. Their hunting grounds stretched southwards into the United States and northwards as far as the North Saskatchewan River. The Rockies were the boundary of their territory to the west, and the Confederacy spread eastward far into present-day Saskatchewan. Although they did not believe that they actually owned this land, they refused to allow other peoples on it: it was their hunting preserve. Neighbouring First Nations were attacked if they trespassed on Blackfoot territory, just as the Blackfoot were attacked if they strayed beyond the limits of the Confederacy's hunting grounds. However, this did not prevent frequent raids into enemy territory for hunting and plunder - and especially for glory.

In these raids, the Blackfoot had a great advantage over their enemies: they were better supplied with guns and horses. Because of their geographical position, they could get horses from the American Fur Company posts on the Missouri, and guns from the Hudson's Bay Company on the North Saskatchewan River. Most First Nations did not have this choice of trading companies and trade goods. The Blackfoot had another great advantage over their neighbours. Because of their reputation for fierceness, very few traders or missionaries ever entered their territory. So their civilization remained intact.

They had, of course, made a few changes in their way of life since first contact with Europeans. They no longer grew tobacco, for it was easier to get it through trade. They used European goods, such as iron kettles, axes, blankets and guns. But they continued to use spears and bows and arrows when hunting buffalo. A musket took too long to reload when a rider was galloping alongside the herds.

Horses had brought the greatest change to Blackfoot life. Besides providing speed and agility in hunting and warfare, they were important as beasts of burden. With horses -

At the Blackfoot Crossing

instead of dogs - to pull the travoises, the Blackfoot could take large quantities of goods from camp to camp. And they no longer had to leave much of the buffalo meat at the scene of a hunt.

By the time Crowfoot was born, the Blackfoot had owned horses for a hundred years. The animals had become part of their lifestyle. They were used like money to buy things, and a man's wealth was reckoned by the size of his herds. The aim of forays was often to capture enemy horses.

Since the animals played such an important role, Blackfoot children were placed on horseback almost as soon as they could walk. Crowfoot would have been a competent rider by the time he was five. By the age of ten, he would have been looking after his stepfather's horse herd, getting up before dawn each day to take the animals to water. As a ten-year-old, he would also have started to ride out on buffalo hunts, learning the techniques from his elders.

The life of the Blackfoot revolved around the buffalo, and they used every part of these shaggy beasts for some purpose. The hairy hides served as bedding or were made into winter clothing. The dressed, hairless skins were made into lighter clothing or used to make tipi covers or ceremonial headdresses. The hair was fashioned into ropes, bridles and ornaments. The rawhide served many purposes and was one of the materials used for waterproof containers. The bones were made into tools; the horns into cups and spoons. And the meat proved the staple food. Berries and roots supplemented the Blackfoot diet, but buffalo meat was the real food. During a hunt, choice portions were eaten raw, but generally the meat was boiled or roasted. If it was to be preserved, it was dried in the sun and either boiled and made into pemmican or simply stored as dried meat.

The women and girls performed most of these household tasks. A young boy like Crowfoot did not have to learn how to tan buffalo hides or preserve food. But, like Blackfoot girls, he was taught to respect his elders and to observe the taboos connected with the sacred medicine bundles. Much of his education was aimed at physical fitness. He played body-building games with other boys of his age, for he was expected to become a strong fighter. His stepfather and the other men of the band carefully trained him toward this goal from early childhood.

Crowfoot's stepfather was called Akay-nehka-simi (Many Names), and he belonged to the Biters band of Blackfoot. And it was among this band that Crowfoot grew up. Each of the First Nations within the Confederacy was divided into a number of bands, which lived separately from each other for most of the year, following the buffalo across the plains during the summer months, and camping in sheltered wooded areas during the winter.

The members of a band were generally related, and the chief acted as a father, seeing that all under his care were protected and well fed. The chief had no official power except his influence - though this could be considerable. If his followers disliked his leadership, they could join another band or form a new one. Blackfoot society was very democratic.

It was a well-ordered society, based on a firm religious faith, a strong moral code, and a real concern for the good of the community. Crowfoot was brought up to practise generosity. The Blackfoot believed that the rich should give to the poor, and that the strong should help the weak. Orphans were fed and clothed. People who were too old or ill to hunt were provided for by healthy young men. Crowfoot was also taught to be a sociable band member, to perform his duties without grumbling, to accept teasing without causing strife,

A Blackfoot camp, 1883

and to be faithful to his people. And a desire for bravery - the greatest manly virtue - was instilled in him from a very early age. Cowardice was despised and ridiculed.

Anyone who did not conform to these high standards was either shamed into better behaviour by ridicule or punished by one of the men's societies. There were several men's societies in the Confederacy, each consisting of people of much the same age. Later, when Crowfoot was a young man, he joined an age-grade society called the All Brave Dogs. Like most other men's societies, the All Brave Dogs were part policemen and part soldiers. They protected the band when it was on the move and took turns at guard duty, acting as sentries to keep watch for enemies. Often they settled minor disputes between fellow Blackfoot.

The Sun Dance was the great religious festival, when the scattered bands of the Confederacy tribes came together to honour the Creator and pray for health and good fortune. It was a very holy ceremony with a complex ritual that took several days to perform. In many respects, the Sun Dance was a statement of all that the Blackfoot believed in - and not only spiritually. This was the occasion when the unity of the Confederacy was confirmed as old friends met up again.

They were most active at the time of the Sun Dance when it was their duty to keep order in camp and to see that each man did his share of hunting, and provided meat for the feasts and buffalo tongues for the ceremonies.

Tribal virtues were emphasized during this festival. Boys like Crowfoot received their greatest inspiration as they sat at the edge of the Sun Dance circle listening to the most daring men recounting their exploits. Glorious battles would be relived to draw the admiration of the audience.

Such long and involved festivals had not been possible before the era of the horse. With horses, the Blackfoot found they had leisure. They had time to develop their culture and hold lengthy religious and social functions. They had time for art and craftsmanship, time for games and sports. And they had time to raid their enemies, not only to gain glory but also to bring back a fresh supply of horses.

The Blackfoot were at the height of their civilization when Crowfoot was a small child. Prosperous and powerful, they were lords of the plains, unthreatened by the hunger that had haunted their ancestors, and unthreatened as yet by the handful of Europeans who lived on their borders. The buffalo were plentiful, and as long as summer followed summer, there seemed no reason that their civilization should not grow from strength to strength.

But the Confederacy experienced the first of many disasters shortly after Crowfoot's mother remarried. First there was an outbreak of diphtheria and then, in 1837, a smallpox

Blackfoot picture writing

epidemic. One Aboriginal caught the disease from a passenger on an American Fur Company steamer on the Missouri, and before long it was sweeping the plains, spreading from First Nation to First Nation. The Blackfoot had no immunity against smallpox, and whole bands died of the disease. Some young men committed suicide when they caught it, rather than suffer the terrible disfigurement it caused. About 6,000 people – two-thirds of the entire Blackfoot nation – died during this epidemic.

Crowfoot was only seven years old at the time, and fortunately he and his family were among the survivors. But it was a sign of what was in store, and the first of many tribulations he would have to face. For Crowfoot was to live through the years of great change, when the buffalo vanished from the prairies and European settlers moved in and the railway spread its line of steel across to the Pacific.

The harm done to the Blackfoot during these years was seldom intentional, no more intentional than the smallpox epidemic. Often it was caused simply by thoughtlessness. Sometimes it was the result of government policy - to do what was best for the European population of Canada. But the result was always the same: to reduce the strength of the Aboriginal people.

Young Crowfoot naturally had no idea of the hard times ahead as he admired his elders at the Sun Dance or wrestled playfully with his friends. He was training to be a soldier. But, even as a youth, he began to exhibit the wisdom and strength of character that enabled him to lead his people - as successfully as was possible - through their most difficult years of social change.

Chapter 2
Years of Glory

Many stories are told about Crowfoot's youth, but the most famous of all is the tale of how he earned the right to take the name Crowfoot. He was a teenager at the time, a junior member of a large party that had set out to attack a Crow camp in Montana. In spite of his youth, he was already a veteran, having taken part in a number of raids - first in the role of servant and horse-minder, and then as a fighter in his own right. But never before had he been the hero of a battle.

Crowfoot's bravery during the raid in Montana drew the admiration of all his companions, for although he was wounded in the attack - shot through the arm by a musket ball and knocked to the ground - he struggled to his feet again and raced forward boldly. Ignoring enemy fire, he broke through the Crow defences and charged into their camp ahead of any of the others. He collapsed shortly afterwards and was helped to safety by his stepbrother, Three Bulls. But his courage had been noted. After the battle, all agreed that he was entitled to claim a hero's name.

He chose Isapo-muxika (Crow Indian's Big Foot). This name had originally belonged to a famous Blackfoot chief who had placed his foot in a large footprint that had been left in the mud by a fleeing Crow warrior. This first Isapo-muxika had performed many heroic deeds before being killed in ambush, so it was fitting that the young Crowfoot should take the name when he had exceptionally distinguished himself.

This story is one of many in which Crowfoot's future greatness was predicted. It is said that, before the battle, the chief of Crowfoot's expedition saw that there was a captured Piegan tipi standing in the Crow camp. He declared that whoever reached the tipi first and struck it with his whip would become the leader of his people in hunting and in war.

Crowfoot, 1887, wearing the owl's head talisman in his hair

Crowfoot struck the tipi first as he charged into the camp ahead of his fellows.

Another story foretelling Crowfoot's leadership describes how he had a dream in which a buffalo spirit came to him and informed him that one day he would be the father of his people. Dreams were taken very seriously for they were one of the ways by which the spirit world was believed to communicate with humans. Young men would go off alone and fast for

several days seeking a dream that would give them

supernatural power and guidance.

Crowfoot was not as religious as some of the Blackfoot. He was a practical man of action rather than a mystic. But he set great store by his dream. He also believed in the power of an owl's head which was given to him by Three Suns, the chief of the Biters band. Crowfoot wore the owl's head in his hair all his life, and it can be seen in many of his photographs. When presenting the talisman, Three Suns told Crowfoot it would protect him, and that he would become a great leader if he wore it. This was not a blind prophecy for Crowfoot had already proved himself a very able fighting man.

Although some of the stories about Crowfoot's early exploits may well have sprung up after he became famous, undoubtedly he did draw attention to himself while still very young. He was not only exceptionally brave; by the time he was in his twenties, he had also gained a reputation for being able to act very wisely.

He acted with unusual wisdom the time he roused the scorn of the All Brave Dogs – the age-grade society to which he belonged – even though the original fault was his. Crowfoot had a violent temper, which flared quickly and which he found hard to control. On this particular occasion, during a skirmish, he and a comrade had grabbed for a fallen enemy's rifle at the same time. Crowfoot lost his temper and refused to let go of the rifle. He insisted he had picked it up first. The other man let him have it. But that night, at the victory dance, he publicly accused Crowfoot of taking the rifle from him, and challenged Crowfoot to stand up and fight for it.

Crowfoot refused to do so. Although his temper was quick, it died down just as quickly, and he knew that no good would come of fighting a fellow member of All Brave Dogs. Either he or his challenger would surely be killed, and this could start a blood feud which would divide the band. So, instead of fighting as was expected, Crowfoot sat quietly in his place while the other All Brave Dogs jeered at him for his cowardice and selfishness.

Moral courage, the courage to do what one knows is right can be far more difficult than physical courage, especially in a society like that of the Blackfoot. Later in life, Crowfoot was to show, time and again, that he had the self-discipline not to fight when fighting would only bring harm to his people.

Nevertheless, anyone as brave as Crowfoot could not have enjoyed being accused of cowardice, even though it did not harm his reputation. For through his twenties and on into his thirties, his courage became legendary. According to Father Albert Lacombe, the great missionary priest, Crowfoot fought in nineteen battles and was wounded six times. He saved Father Lacombe's life in one of these battles. This was in December 1865, when the priest was visiting a Blackfoot camp. During the night it was attacked by the Cree, as Father Lacombe relates.

Exhausted by fatigue, I was quietly sleeping in the tent of the chief when...suddenly a dog put his head into the lodge. It was a Cree dog...The alarm was given. In one second the Crees who were watching about a hundred yards off opened fire. In an instant some score of bullets came crashing through the leather lodge and the wild war-whoop of the Crees broke forth through the sharp and rapid detonation of many muskets. It is not my intention to give here the awful details of that fearful night when the groans of the dying, the yelling of the warriors, the harangues of the chiefs, and the noise of dogs and horses all mingled formed a kind of hell. I have only to say that at the most critical moment when our little camp was half taken by the Crees and when scalping and butchering were going on, the voice of Crowfoot was heard. He was rushing to our rescue. "Ekakimak" (Take courage) he cried out as he came with a large party of warriors. We were saved.

What Father Lacombe does not say in this account is that he also acted very bravely that night. He was known to the Cree since he had already worked among them as a missionary, and he thought that if he went out into the open between the two opposing forces he might be able to stop the battle. But the Cree could not recognize the priest in the dark and they went on firing. A bullet ricocheted off a rock and grazed Father Lacombe's head knocking him to the ground. The Blackfoot carried him into a lodge and the fighting continued with increasing desperation until Crowfoot's band routed the Cree attackers.

Crowfoot was about 35 years old at this time and one of the most respected men in the tribe. He was a living example

of the Blackfoot ideal: brave in war, kind to the needy and extremely generous. This must have been one of the happiest periods of his life. His success as warrior and hunter had brought him wealth and he owned a great many horses. He had a growing family of children and several wives. The first and favourite of whom was Sisoyaki (Cutting Woman). In addition he had a large following; although not yet a chief he was certainly a leader.

The chief of the Biters had died that year and the band divided into two groups. Just over half decided to follow Three Suns, the son and namesake of the old chief. But 21 lodges preferred Crowfoot as their leader, and they formed a

Father Lacombe trying to stop a battle between Cree and Blackfoot

separate group which became known as the Big Pipes.

The following year, 1866, Crowfoot was accepted as a chief not only by his band but by the entire Blackfoot nation. The bands had gathered for the Sun Dance. Some women who were picking berries for the ceremony were harassed by a grizzly bear which mauled the lad who was on duty to protect them. The women fled for help - and out to the rescue rode the All Brave Dogs.

Crowfoot was not the leader of the All Brave Dogs but he seems to have taken charge on this occasion, telling the others to attract the attention of the angry grizzly and entice it towards them while he came up on it from behind. When the huge beast was tempted forward out of the bushes, Crowfoot rode after it and killed it singlehanded, plunging his spear into the beast again and again until it was dead. This incredible act of bravery was witnessed by a large portion of the Blackfoot nation. Grizzlies were considered to have supernatural powers in addition to their great physical strength, so Crowfoot's bravery was doubly impressive. From then on he was regarded as a chief of great note.

Crowfoot's band later became known as the Moccasins.

Crowfoot increased his prestige later the same year in an incident involving the Hudson's Bay Company. The head chief of the Bloods, Seen From Afar had invited a party of traders from Fort Edmonton to come to do business with him. Accordingly John Cunningham, a Hudson's Bay Company clerk, set out south into Blackfoot territory with a caravan of Red River carts. When he arrived at Seen From Afar's camp he found a great gathering of Bloods, Blackfoot, Piegans, and Sarcees - many of whom were extremely hostile. Seen From Afar smoked with Cunningham as a symbol of friendship, as did Crowfoot and some other chiefs. Most of the Blackfoot chiefs did not smoke. The powerful Blackfoot chief, Big Swan, was especially hostile. He made a speech attacking the traders and then began looting their goods. Seen From Afar tried to stop him, insisting that the men were his guests and must not be harmed. Tempers were running high and there were more Blackfoot than Blood present. Cunningham began to fear for his life.

At this point Crowfoot stepped forward and stood boldly beside the Blood chief. He turned furiously on Big Swan and hurled insults at him. Big Swan was far senior to Crowfoot.

He was one of the most powerful Blackfoot chiefs. And he had many of his followers with him. Crowfoot had a strong sense of honour and was not prepared to stand by to watch invited guests massacred. His outburst had its effect. Several other chiefs joined Crowfoot and Seen From Afar, and escorted Cunningham safely away.

By rights, Crowfoot should have lost face over this incident for he had sided with a Blood leader against his fellow Blackfoot. Instead, because he had acted with such courage, risking his life for the sake of his principles, his reputation increased.

In 1832 the population of the Blackfoot was esti-mated to be about 4,500.

A few years after this episode, another outbreak of small-pox within the Confederacy killed Three Suns, the chief of the Biters band. Automatically Crowfoot became chief of the Biters, as well as of his own Big Pipes band. In 1872, Big Swan died of tuberculosis. This left Crowfoot and a chief named Old Sun as the two leading chiefs of the Blackfoot nation. Crowfoot had a following of about 1,300 people, while Old Sun had about 800 followers. As a head chief of the Blackfoot, Crowfoot was recognized as one of the most influential men in the entire Blackfoot Confederacy.

A Red River cart

Poundmaker, 1886

Unfortunately, his first years as head chief were marred by sadness. His teenage son, his only healthy son, went out to war and did not return. He was shot by a band of Cree. Crowfoot was shattered by the loss - and burning with anger. He was no longer young, nor was he strong and agile, for he had been weakened by a bullet that had lodged in his leg some years earlier and had never been removed. Nevertheless, he was determined to avenge his son's death in person. With a personally selected group of companions, he set out to attack a Cree camp. Only one Cree was killed in the raid, but Crowfoot considered this sufficient revenge to satisfy his honour. His anger had passed, and he had no wish to cause widespread destruction.

Shortly after this, the Cree and Blackfoot made peace. Crowfoot visited a Cree camp and came across a young man who looked remarkably like his dead son. His name was Seka-kinyan (Poundmaker). He was older than Crowfoot's son had been, but Crowfoot was impressed by his personality as well as by his uncanny resemblance to the dead teenager. When he heard that Poundmaker had no close family of his own alive, Crowfoot invited the young Cree to join the Blackfoot camp, and later adopted him as a son. Even when fighting again broke out between the tribes, Poundmaker stayed on with Crowfoot.

When Poundmaker eventually returned to his own people, Crowfoot loaded him with gifts. But Poundmaker took more than material goods with him. During the months he had been with Crowfoot, he had absorbed much of the chief's philosophy. Like Crowfoot, he had often hoped for peace between First Nations, and this desire had been strengthened as he came under Crowfoot's influence. During the years that followed, the two men met whenever possible, working together to bring peace to the plains.

Although Crowfoot had grown up in a warlike environment, his instinct had always been to prevent bloodshed. True, he would be first in the fray when his people were in danger. He was prepared to fight to the death to protect his band. Similarly, he would take retaliatory measures when he felt they were necessary. And he would not stop his men from raiding enemy camps in times of war. Crowfoot himself had given up offensive warfare when he was about twenty. Basically he was a peace-loving man. When treaties had been signed, he kept a tight rein on his warriors, restraining them from making surprise attacks on enemy camps. This was no easy task, for the younger men were always eager to gain glory.

Crowfoot had great influence. He could make brilliant speeches that would persuade the most stubborn to follow his advice. He was an extremely eloquent orator. His authority was seldom questioned. But he did not simply inspire respect. Very often he commanded it. Crowfoot did not like being argued with, and, if anyone opposed him, he could fly into one of his rages. Once he set on a group of Blood warriors (who were not even under his leadership) because they ignored him when he told them to stop pillaging some traders. "If you people are going to trade," he shouted angrily, "you must be fair!" He was outraged at their lack of honour.

Crowfoot believed passionately in honour and justice. Until a man proved himself an enemy, Crowfoot was prepared to treat him as a friend. This attitude made him very popular with the Hudson's Bay Company traders. They observed his growing influence with relief, for some of the other chiefs were not so well-intentioned. Many of them resented the traders and their forts. Crowfoot bore the company men no ill will, and he appreciated the goods they supplied.

But this era of the Hudson's Bay Company was coming to an end. The company was about to sell all of Rupert's Land

and the North-West Territories to the government. Crowfoot was unaware that the company owned this land, so the sale would have made no sense to him even if he had been informed of it. Land ownership was a European concept that was foreign to Aboriginal peoples. No one person could own land any more than one could own the sky or the sun. Nevertheless, in 1869, the Hudson's Bay Company arranged to sell the government vast areas of northwestern Canada, which included the traditional hunting grounds of the Blackfoot Confederacy. The effects began to be felt almost immediately, causing trouble to Crowfoot, and strife among his people.

Chapter 3
The Coming of the Red Coats

The Hudson's Bay Company followed a very careful policy during the years it had held a monopoly over trade in the North-West. Company clerks were picked men, and they were expected to maintain a high standard of conduct, especially in their behaviour towards Aboriginal peoples. One of the rules of the company stated:

That the Indians be treated with kindness and indulgence, and mild and conciliatory means resorted to in order to encourage industry, repress vice, and inculcate morality; that the use of spiritous liquors be gradually discontinued in the very few districts in which it is yet indispensable; and that the Indians be liberally supplied with requisite necessaries, particularly with articles of ammunition, whether they have the means of paying for it or not.

The use of spiritous liquors was discontinued and the company took pains to remain on good terms with the First Nations, and on the whole, was successful. Even when the Blackfoot were battling with the Americans, they continued to trade the goods they pillaged from the American posts at the Hudson's Bay Company.

Blackfoot relations with the Americans had been far from amicable over the years, with an unfortunate beginning: two Piegans were killed when the Lewis and Clark expedition first entered Blackfoot territory in 1806. This caused the Confederacy to look on all Long Knives (as they called the Americans) as enemies. Half a century later, even though trading was vigorous, there were still sporadic outbreaks of violence. Sometimes an Aboriginal would be murdered; sometimes one of the Long Knives. There was little friendship between the two groups.

Part of the problem was that there was no general policy

Fort Whoop-Up

of behaviour as there was in Canada. Although some of the American traders were men of principle, others were adventurers who were out to get rich quickly.

They found they could make the greatest profit by trading liquor for buffalo robes, and that is what they did, even though it was illegal. There was little law enforcement in the American West - and there was a great demand for buffalo robes. One manufacturer discovered that the hides were tough enough to make leather belts to be used in factory machinery. The market for them was limitless. The liquor trade flourished in spite of the harm it did. Fortunately most of the Confederacy bands lived too far north to suffer greatly from the trade. Generally they hunted in Canada where the Hudson's Bay Company held sway, and where no liquor traders were allowed. All this changed when the North-West was sold to the Dominion government. Company rule came to an end, and the territory was wide open to anyone who chose to enter it. Soon ambitious Americans were moving across the border and establishing trading posts in Canada.

The most notorious of these was Fort Whoop-Up, built in 1869 by the two profiteers John J. Healy and Alfred B. Hamilton.

Like the other trading forts, Whoop-Up supplied a variety of goods, but it made its greatest profits from repeating rifles and liquor. Both had a destructive effect. The repeating rifle made hunting so easy that buffalo were slaughtered by the thousand - for their hides rather than the meat. Meanwhile, the sudden flow of liquor caused havoc among the Confederacy. The camps became drunk and disorderly, and 88 people died one year as the result of brawls. Even Crowfoot found it hard to control his followers. There was trouble with the traders too. They shot at the Aboriginals on the slightest provocation; the Aboriginals retaliated by burning some of their forts.

Crowfoot was appalled by the effects of the liquor trade on his people. The whole fabric of Blackfoot culture seemed to be falling apart. Many of his fellow chiefs were worried too, for their traditional enemies were quick to take advantage of the Confederacy's weakness. The Cree, who were too far north to be affected, were moving boldly into areas that for generations had been Blackfoot hunting territory. Meanwhile, the fighting between First Nations and traders was increasing. It came to a head in 1873 when a group of American and Canadian wolf hunters massacred about 30 Assinibois in the Cypress Hills.

This was the event that finally forced the Dominion government to take action. The government had been growing increasingly anxious as reports came in of lawlessness in the West, and of American infiltration. Obviously order had to be established, and the whisky forts closed. Many traders blatantly flew the American flag from these forts, regardless of the fact that they were operating illegally in Canada. Already, by the time of the Cypress Hills massacre, a bill had been passed in Parliament establishing the North-West Mounted Police. Unfortunately the wheels of government had been moving slowly. Only when news of the massacre reached Ottawa did recruiting begin in earnest.

The Reverend John McDougall (son of the missionary George McDougall) went ahead into Blackfoot territory to prepare the way for the Mounted Police. He already knew

Healy later became a sheriff and Hamilton became a member of the Montana legislature.

The missionary, Constantine Scollen, gives a depressing picture of the Blackfoot Confederacy at this time:

The fiery water flowed as freely, if I may use the metaphor, as the streams running from the Rock Mountains, and hundreds of the poor Indians fell victims to the white man's craving for money, some poisoned, some frozen to death whilst in the state of intoxication, and many shot down by American bullets. Then in 1870 came that disease so fatal to Indians, the smallpox, which told upon the Blackfeet with terrible effect, destroying between 600 and 800 of them. Surviving relatives went more and more for the use of alcohol; they endeavoured to drown their grief in the poisonous beverage. They sold their robes and their horses by the hundred for it, and now they began killing one another, so that in a short time they were divided into several small parties, afraid to meet. It was painful to me to see the state of poverty to which they had been reduced. Formerly they had been the most opulent Indians in the country, and now they were clothed in rags, without horses and without guns.

John McDougall

several of the Confederacy chiefs, and, early in 1874, he had a meeting with Crowfoot to tell him who the Mounties were and why they were coming. Crowfoot said they would be welcome if they would stop the whisky trade. He was pleased by McDougall's descriptions of British justice. If the "Queen's soldiers" treated all people equally, as McDougall said, then Crowfoot was willing to allow them to build forts in Blackfoot territory. The other chiefs agreed.

When the Mounted Police arrived in the autumn of 1874, they went straight into action against the whisky traders. Many had already fled, while others had disposed of their liquor, but there were some who still tried to carry on the trade illicitly. These men were sought out and prosecuted. Their liquor was spilled and their goods confiscated. Those who could not pay the fines imposed on them were put under guard, though there was as yet no guardhouse to put them in .

*Lieutenant-Colonel
James F. Macleod*

The Mounted Police were showing they meant business, even before they had time to build Fort MacLeod.

Crowfoot observed their behaviour with approval, and his respect for the Red Coats increased as the months passed. As McDougall had promised, they did indeed treat traders and Aboriginals impartially. Crowfoot was particularly impressed by the careful manner in which Lieutenant-Colonel Macleod examined the evidence before passing sentence on anyone. James Farquharson Macleod was assistant-commissioner of the Force and senior officer in the region. From the first, Crowfoot felt a common bond with him. Here was a fellow leader who also believed in justice. Crowfoot was prepared to work with him and support his efforts to establish law and peace on the plains.

With this end in view, he forbade his warriors to raid enemy camps. When some of them did go on raiding parties,

NWMP encampment

he returned the horses they had taken. This was against all tradition, but Crowfoot knew that it was necessary if the peoples of the plains were to live in peace. He preferred to give his men some of his own horses, rather than let them keep the ones they had stolen. However, most agreed to stop their raids. Now that liquor was no longer firing their aggressiveness, they once again listened to Crowfoot and yielded to his authority.

It was a return to the old order. The very moral code of Blackfoot behaviour was re-established. Buffalo hides were once more used to make clothing, or buy food and other necessities. The Confederacy once again became prosperous and industrious.

Chapter 4
The Settlers and the Sioux

Thanks to the Mounted Police, and to chiefs like Crowfoot and Poundmaker, the western plains soon became more peaceful than they had ever been before. But this brought new problems. Now that the tribes were no longer warring among themselves, the prairies were an attractive region for settlement.

Homesteaders began to move in. There were only a few at first, but Crowfoot was quick to realize the significance. He knew that they could be expected in ever-increasing numbers. Meanwhile, lawful American traders were coming into Blackfoot territory from the south and forming fairly large settlements in the hunting grounds along the Belly River. From the north too came the Cree and Metis, who no longer feared Blackfoot attacks now that they were protected by the Mounted Police. The Confederacy was being hemmed in from all sides.

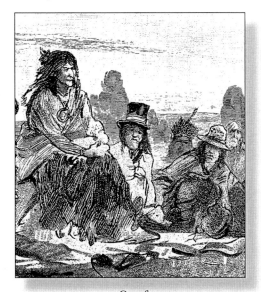

Crowfoot at a council meeting

Crowfoot became anxious. He saw something had to be done to protect his people. Buffalo were scarcer than they had been, and the herds were less easy to find. He could not afford to let outsiders move into good hunting areas. So he called a council meeting of all the bands of the Confederacy to discuss their common problems and decide on a course of action. The chiefs drafted a document which the interpreter, Jean L'Heureux, copied out for them and sent to the lieutenant-governor of the North-West Territories. It was a very lucid statement, explaining the problems the Confederacy was facing and asking for a meeting with a representative of "our Great Mother, Her Majesty the Queen," so that a solution could be found. No Queen's representative visited the Blackfoot, but eventually they were informed that the government was willing to arrange a treaty with them.

The First Nations were divided about the idea of a treaty. Crowfoot was eager for one because he saw that something had to be done to control the invasion of Blackfoot territory by so many different groups of people. And he knew that the buffalo would not last forever. Each year there were fewer, just as each year the number of settlers grew. He wanted an agreement that would protect his people in these changing circumstances.

Many chiefs supported Crowfoot, and they became all the more eager when the government made a treaty with the Cree in 1876. They felt that the Cree were being favoured. The southern bands of the Confederacy were suspicious, especially the Piegans. They knew all about treaties. Most of the Piegan bands hunted south of the 49th parallel, and as "American" Nations, they had signed the Judith Treaty with the United States government in 1855. A few other Confederacy chiefs had also signed this treaty. They had bitterly regretted doing so.

The Judith Treaty was intended to stop the liquor trade, but the trade had continued. It had guaranteed to protect the Blackfoot from attacks by Long Knives. Yet Blackfoot continued to be killed from time to time, and the murderers were not prosecuted. The treaty had recognized thousands of square kilometres of Aboriginal hunting grounds just south of the Canadian border. But in 1862, immigrants poured in when gold was discovered in these hunting grounds at Grasshopper Creek. In the disputes which followed, the police continually sided against the First Nations.

Disputes were common, for the recent wave of immigrants and settlers was a ruffian lot. As the Indian Superintendent of Montana sadly reported, "There is a white element in this country which from its rowdy and lawless character cannot be excelled in any section." As might be expected, the First Nations hit back, conducting a series of guerrilla attacks on the settlers. The settlers demanded protection - and revenge. They got both.

In 1870, four troops of United States cavalry and 55

mounted infantrymen were sent to put down what had become known as the "Blackfeet War." By mistake, they attacked a peaceful Piegan camp which had taken no part in the hostilities and was stricken with smallpox at the time. One of the chiefs actually went out to greet the troops unarmed. He was shot down and killed. A terrible massacre followed and the camp was wiped out. Hundreds of Piegans were wounded, and 173 women and children were slaughtered.

The members of the Confederacy who lived near enough to have heard of these events first-hand rather naturally had little faith in treaties. Moreover, the Sioux had been having similar troubles. The Sioux had made a treaty with the United States government in 1868. A few years later, gold was discovered in their allotted hunting grounds. When they were ordered out of the gold-mining areas and onto their reserves, the great Sioux chief, Sitting Bull, decided to fight.

Chief Sitting Bull

Sitting Bull needed all the allies he could find, and he even approached his traditional enemies in the hope that they would join forces with him. He sent a peace offering of tobacco to Crowfoot and said he would help Crowfoot rid himself of the Red Coats if Crowfoot would help him conquer the Long Knives. Crowfoot had no wish to turn on Macleod and the Mounted Police. He greatly appreciated their work. In any case, it was not in his nature to repay friendship with treachery. Nor did he particularly wish to fight the Americans. He already suspected that the power of all these newcomers was far stronger than it appeared to be from the relatively small numbers who had come to the West. Open warfare could bring the Blackfoot nothing but harm.

Crowfoot could not speak for the whole Confederacy until he had consulted with the other head chiefs, but they too declined to support their Sioux enemies. Crowfoot sent word to Sitting Bull that the Blackfoot would not join him. Sitting Bull's answer was that after he had massacred the Long Knives, he would come to Canada to massacre the Mounted Police and the Blackfoot.

Cecil Denny, a Mounted Police officer, was in camp when Crowfoot received this disturbing reply. He assured Crowfoot that the Mounted Police would protect the Blackfoot if the Sioux attacked them. Crowfoot, in turn, promised that if the Red Coats were attacked, he would raise 2,000 men in their defence. He made a moving speech during which he pledged his loyalty to Queen Victoria and called upon her to ensure his people would not be allowed to starve when the buffalo vanished from the plains. Eventually the gist of his speech reached the queen, and in due course a grateful reply was sent to Crowfoot.

Both London and Ottawa hailed Crowfoot for his "loyalty". But Crowfoot's loyalties were where they had always been - with his own people. Throughout his life, the ruling factor in all his decisions was to do what was best for his band, his tribe, his Confederacy and his fellow Aboriginals. That was why he was prepared to make peace with Sitting Bull when the Sioux fled into Canada after the Battle of Little Big Horn.

The Sioux won the battle, but they were not equipped to sustain a full-scale war against the United States forces. They arrived in Canada as refugees. As such, they needed the friendship of the Canadian First Nations as well as that of the Mounted Police. Most of the Blackfoot were willing to drive the Sioux back across the American border. Not only were the Sioux long-standing enemies, they were also noted buffalo hunters and would further reduce the dwindling number of buffalo available to the Blackfoot. Crowfoot counselled

Fort Macleod

against war. He did not want to see Aboriginal blood once again flowing across the plains. When Sitting Bull sent Crowfoot a gift of tobacco as a peace offering, he cautiously agreed to meet the Sioux leader, and received Sitting Bull as a guest in his lodge. The two chiefs smoked together and held a friendship dance.

The motives of both men were constructive and peaceable, but when Montana citizens heard of the conference, they became alarmed. They assumed that Sitting Bull was gathering allies for another campaign. Even the Canadian government grew anxious. Perhaps the Blackfoot would join the Sioux and resort to war after all. Obviously, the sooner the Blackfoot were bound by treaty to the Canadian government, the better it would be for all.

Chapter 5
Treaty Number Seven

Colonel Macleod and Lieutenant-Governor David Laird were the commissioners appointed to arrange the Blackfoot treaty (to include the Stoney peoples and any other First Nations of the plains who had not yet ceded their land to the government). The two commissioners suggested a meeting in September 1877 at Fort Macleod. Crowfoot did not like the idea of negotiating in a government fort. He chose a different location: Blackfoot Crossing on the Bow River, in his own hunting grounds.

During September the various parties duly began to assemble at Blackfoot Crossing. Crowfoot and the other Blackfoot chiefs arrived with their bands. Representatives of the Stoney First Nations arrived and camped on the other side of the river - for they were old enemies of the Blackfoot. Various missionaries and interpreters arrived. Lieutenant-Governor Laird arrived. Colonel Macleod arrived with 80 officers of the Mounted Police. Even Mrs. Macleod came, as did Mrs. McDougall and a few other women. But most of the Blood, Piegan and Sarcee bands did not come. They did not approve of the change in location. Blackfoot Crossing was not a central and neutral place like Fort Macleod. The people felt the commissioners were favouring Crowfoot.

In 1986 the Canadian Post Office issued a pair of stamps honouring Crowfoot and Macleod.

They had some justification, because the Mounted Police frequently treated Crowfoot as if he were the ruler of the entire Blackfoot nation, when in fact he was only chief of one band, or, at best, a leading chief of the Blackfoot Nation. Certainly Crowfoot had great influence, but there were chiefs in the Blood tribe who had a greater number of followers and just as much influence. These chiefs resented his preferential treatment.

The treaty looked as if it was doomed to failure before the terms had even been discussed. It would not be worth much unless all the First Nations agreed to it. The commissioners were in an awkward position: Lieutenant-Governor Laird had travelled more than 1,100 km to meet with the chiefs. He could hardly return without a treaty.

Laird decided to postpone the proceedings for a couple of days and, as a sign of good will, he offered those who were present rations of flour, tea, sugar, tobacco and beef. Crowfoot refused them. He did not want to accept any gifts until he had heard the terms offered. Many other chiefs followed his example. This made Laird and Macleod even more anxious. If Crowfoot rejected the treaty, the rest of the Confederacy would probably do so too.

During the next two days many Sarcees joined the camp, and some Piegans. The assembly looked huge, camped in separate groups along the Bow River, but it was not complete. The important Blood chiefs and their followers had still not come.

Most of the Piegan bands were not affected, since they hunted farther south and were considered to be "American".

Nevertheless, Laird called a formal meeting on Wednesday, 19 September; he announced the terms of the treaty. The First Nations would cede about 130,000 km 2 of land to the government, though hunting would be allowed to continue in this area so long as they did not "molest settlers and others in the country." Each nation would be granted a reserve, the size of each being proportioned according to population figures: over two square kilometres would be allowed for each family of five. When each nation eventually settled on its reserves, the government would provide it with schools and other services.

The treaty also guaranteed to spend $2,000 a year on supplying the First Nations with ammunition. It promised annual cash payments of $25 to leading chiefs, $15 to minor chiefs, and $5 to every man, woman and child. In addition, each chief would receive a suit of clothes every three years.

There were several other clauses, some dealing specifically with the Stoney peoples, but on the whole the terms were the same as those that the Cree had accepted the previous year. One main difference was that the Blackfoot were offered cattle as an alternative to farming implements because ranching was more in their tradition than agriculture.

Lieutenant-Governor Laird did not expect an immediate reply to his offer. He did hope to receive an acceptance at the meeting he called the following day. He was disappointed. Crowfoot said he was not yet ready to give an answer. Most of the chiefs took their lead from him and also remained silent. Only one Blackfoot and leaders of the Stoney First Nation spoke out in favour of the treaty. Those Bloods who were present were strongly opposed to it.

The big problem was that the treaty did not settle the Confederacy's troubles. On the contrary. Confederacy chiefs complained that Cree, Metis and various settlers were moving into some of their best hunting grounds, and rather than preventing these actions, the treaty made such encroachments legal. The Blackfoot would receive compensation for the territory they were giving up, but was this enough, in light of the increasing encroachment on their hunting grounds?

Crowfoot was not sure. It was a tough decision for him, especially as he knew that his answer would sway a majority of chiefs. Crowfoot did not want to allow the Cree, Metis or anyone else to hunt on land that the Blackfoot had defended for generations. It would seem like a betrayal of his people even if the buffalo were not so scarce. With the dwindling herds, Crowfoot felt he might well be condemning his people to starvation by allowing others to settle and hunt on their territory.

On the other hand, Crowfoot knew that the days of buffalo hunting were coming to an end: the Blackfoot might face starvation even if they refused to cede their land. What use were vast hunting grounds if there were no buffalo? The treaty at least offered a means of survival. The Blackfoot would become dependent on the government, but Crowfoot did not believe Canadians would act like the Long Knives - whatever the Piegans feared. The Mounted Police had proved to be honest and respectful, and had shown a real concern for the Blackfoot peoples. Crowfoot felt he could trust such men.

He favoured the treaty, but before coming to a decision he wanted to discuss the terms with Red Crow, the astute and powerful Blood chief. Red Crow and his followers were still absent and the mood in camp was getting dangerous. Those in favour of the treaty wanted to sign immediately so that they could receive the special treaty payment of $12 a head. Those opposed were becoming hostile to the commissioners, and some were threatening violence.

Red Crow, head chief of the Blood peoples

It was a difficult time for Crowfoot. He knew trouble was brewing. He also knew that all the bands of all the First Nations would have to agree on the terms if the treaty was to be of practical use.

Finally Crowfoot heard that the Bloods were approaching the meeting sites. It was nearly a week after the date set for the discussions, and the Blood had decided to overlook Crowfoot's preferential treatment. They would take part in the negotiations. When Red Crow arrived, Crowfoot invited him into his lodge. The two powerful leaders sat up all night discussing treaty terms. No one will ever know what was said that night, but by morning Red Crow had made up his mind. He held a meeting with his chiefs to gain their approval.

Then he announced that the Bloods would be willing to sign the treaty – although he said he would leave the final decision to Crowfoot.

This was the assurance Crowfoot needed. At the great gathering that afternoon, Crowfoot spoke first, giving his long-awaited decision to the commissioners. His words have been translated as follows:

While I speak, be kind and patient. I have to speak for my people, who are numerous, and who rely upon me to follow that course which in the future will tend to their good. The plains are large and wide. We are the children of the plains, it is our home, and the buffalo has been our food always. I hope you look upon the Blackfeet, Bloods and Sarcees as your children now, and that you will be indulgent and charitable to them. They all expect me to speak now for them, and I trust the Great Spirit will put into their breasts to be a good people - into the minds of the men, women and children, and their future generations. The advice given me and my people has proved to be very good. If the Police had not come to the country, where would we all be now? Bad men and whisky were killing us so fast that very few of us would have been left today. The Police have protected us as the feathers of a bird protect it from the frosts of winter. I wish them all good, and trust that all our hearts will increase in goodness from this time forward. I am satisfied. I will sign the treaty.

As, one by one, the other chiefs rose to speak, they all took their lead from Crowfoot. "I will sign with Crowfoot," said Red Crow. "We all agree with Crowfoot," said Old Sun. "I agree with Crowfoot, and will sign," said another. Even the war chiefs, who had been arguing against the treaty during the past week, decided that they too would sign with Crowfoot.

The following day a signing ceremony was held, and the leading chiefs were presented with flags, uniforms and medals. Then they formally shook hands with the commissioners while the police band played "God Save the Queen."

During the next few days the treaty payments were made, and sites chosen for reserves. Most of the chiefs were not very interested in their reserves. They had always lived by hunting across the plains, and could not really believe that a time would come when they would be unable to do so. Only Crowfoot seems to have realized that, one day, the reserves

would become the homelands of his people.

He wanted the Confederacy to remain united, so he asked that a large area of land along the Bow River be set aside as the reserve of the Blood, Blackfoot and Sarcee. Crowfoot would have liked the Piegan bands to have their reserve there too, however they chose a reserve farther south on the Oldman River.

The location of the reserves was duly recorded. And so, with everything signed and settled, Treaty Number Seven came into being. An account of the proceedings was later printed in the Toronto Globe, and once again Crowfoot was presented to the Canadian public as a great leader working for peace and unity in the West - as indeed he was. Yet within six months, Crowfoot would come to regret the concessions he had made.

Negotiating Treaty Number 7. Crowfoot is standing at the right. Seated under the canopy are Lieutenant-Colonel Macleod and Lieutenant-Governor Laird. On Macleod's left is interpreter, Jean L'Heureux.

Chapter 6

Troubled Times

Treaty Number 7 reserves. By the terms of the treaty, the Blood and Sarcee reserves were to be on the Bow River alongside the Blackfoot Reserve. The Bloods, however, chose a more southerly site, and later the Sarcees also asked for a separate reserve.

It was unfortunate that the winter immediately following the treaty was a mild one. Prairie fires swept the plains, destroying the grass and preventing the buffalo herds from moving west towards the foothills of the Rockies as usual. Crowfoot had to take his band a long way east before he could provide them with buffalo meat. Already the starvation that he dreaded was threatening his people.

By summer, the grass had grown again and the buffalo had returned. But Crowfoot was worried. The herds were smaller than they used to be and far more scattered. And they were being hunted by people in addition to the members of the Confederacy. The treaty allowed this, and Crowfoot was determined to abide by the treaty. But it was not pleasant for him to see other First Nations in Blackfoot territory, killing buffalo that could well have supported his own people.

Then, in midsummer 1878, Crowfoot learned that the Bloods would have a separate reserve. Red Crow had decided he preferred a more southerly site along the Belly River, and Colonel Macleod had not pressed him to take the region allotted to him in the treaty. Like Crowfoot, Macleod realized that the Confederacy would be less of a political power in the future if each nation lived apart. It was in Macleod's interest to divide the Confederacy.

Crowfoot flew into a violent rage when he heard of the change in plans. He accused Macleod of going back on his word. Crowfoot was so angry that he insulted the colonel publicly, shouting with fury. He apologized the following day. Crowfoot always patched up a quarrel as soon as he cooled down. But he did not change his opinion. Nor did he stop worrying. By signing the treaty, he had handed over much of his power to the Mounted Police. If they abused it, there was little he would be able to do.

The following winter was another hungry one for the Blackfoot as they scoured the plains in search of the few remaining buffalo herds. Food became so scarce that this proud race of hunters was reduced to eating rabbits, gophers and mice. They even ate their dogs. By the spring of 1879, the Blackfoot were starving. Crowfoot sent a message to Battleford, asking for government aid, and that summer the Indian Commissioner, Edgar Dewdney, arrived at Blackfoot Crossing with a great load of food supplies. These could not last forever, and by September the Blackfoot were once again on the verge of starvation.

What was Crowfoot to do? In the north, Poundmaker was reluctantly leading his starving band to their reserve, determined to make a success of farming. There were still buffalo in the south. Just across the American border the buffalo were said to be grazing by the thousand. In fact, American hide-hunters had started prairie fires to block off the herds and prevent them moving north into Canada. Many

Buffalo hunt

bands of the Confederacy had already crossed the border into Montana in search of buffalo. Crowfoot decided he had no choice. His band would have to do the same.

Montana settlers were not pleased when they heard that the powerful Crowfoot had brought his people into their state. They did not believe he was a man of peace. They said he had been responsible for many murders. Crowfoot did nothing to justify this reputation during the years he remained in the United States. Naturally he made no attack on the settlers. It would have been against his whole philosophy to do so. Nor did he allow his followers to raid other Native camps.

This was not easy, because the atmosphere in Montana was tense. Many hereditary enemies had travelled to Montana in search of the buffalo. A group of Cree stole some horses from Crowfoot's camp. Crowfoot forbade his young men to retaliate. He was determined to keep the peace. He even managed to restrain his men one night when they noticed some Cree warriors intent on another raid creeping stealthily towards the camp. Instead of killing the raiders, Crowfoot fearlessly went out alone into the dark - an easy mark if the attackers had decided to shoot him. They did not shoot. They were too surprised. Crowfoot courteously invited them into his lodge, telling them that the days of fighting were over.

Crowfoot had tried to live at peace with the Cree ever since his adoption of Poundmaker. Now he found a Cree chief who became his friend. Big Bear, leader of the largest band of Cree, had taken his people to Montana where they camped nearby Crowfoot's band. Big Bear and Crowfoot formed a lasting friendship, as both chiefs strove to restrain the more hot-blooded members of their bands.

Meanwhile the buffalo hunting continued and, for a time at any rate, the people ate well. But the herds began to quickly diminish with so many hunters in the same area. American ranchers began to complain that the "British Indians" were stealing their cattle. This was undoubtedly true. But some of the ranchers were also raiding the Aboriginal camps and stealing horses. Relations between the two groups, which had been bad from the start, worsened as the months passed. In addition, the various Aboriginal bands fought with each other, raiding for horses, and competing for the remaining buffalo, and they were also drinking heavily. Liquor was available again.

The situation must have seemed like a return to the past, for Crowfoot. Liquor flowed freely. Many of the men selling it were the same people who had been driven from Canada by the Mounted Police. Now they visited the camps in Montana openly, eagerly collecting any goods they were offered. As before, horses and buffalo robes were traded for whisky instead of for the food needed so urgently. Once again, chiefs lost control of their warriors, able to do little more than watch sadly while their tribes disintegrated. The Blackfoot became poorer and hungrier month by month

Crowfoot must have bitterly regretted coming to Montana, though the move had seemed sensible at the time. He led his band even farther south, to the Musselshell River in search of more buffalo. When his hunters returned empty-handed, Crowfoot knew that there was only one way to save his people. He would have to take them back to their reserve in Canada. The treaty payments were being kept for them, and at least they would be provided with food on the reserve.

Returning home was not easy: the Blackfoot had very few horses left. A great many had been lost through theft, and others had been traded. Very few of Crowfoot's people were strong enough to make the journey on foot. They were all suffering from hunger.

One day, a Blackfoot hunting party rode into camp with 70 horses. At last, here was the means of travelling home. But Crowfoot was horrified. The horses had been stolen from the Crow reserve. And the Crow had obviously stolen some from settlers, as many of the horses bore brand marks. Crowfoot knew it was not safe to keep the animals. He insisted on returning them, and it was just as well he did. Several companies of United States cavalry had already received orders to get the horses back and to "move those Indians or bury them."

Crowfoot saved his people from certain destruction, but he was not thanked for this wise behaviour. His young warriors despised him for giving up the animals without a fight. They blamed him openly. They believed they would not have lacked horses in the first place if he had let them retaliate against raiding parties. Crowfoot's band trailed slowly back to Canada on foot, and these young firebrands caused constant trouble. They defied Crowfoot whenever possible and stirred up resentment against him.

It was a terrible and desperate journey. There were so few horses, only the sick and crippled could ride. Crowfoot marched at the tail of the column, encouraging the hopeless, sharing his meagre supplies with those who had none, and setting an example to all by his fortitude and stoicism. In spite of his efforts, many Blackfoot died on the march - some from starvation, others from measles and scarlet fever. It was a sadly weakened band of people who eventually straggled onto the reserve in July of 1881.

Some six weeks after their arrival, Canada's governor general, the Marquis of Lorne, paid the Blackfoot a state visit on his tour of the West. He was the husband of Princess Louise, and was introduced to Crowfoot as "The Great Mother's son-in-law." Four years earlier, at the signing of the treaty, Lieutenant-Governor Laird had been introduced to Crowfoot as "The Great Father." In these few years, between meeting the "father" and son-in-law, the Blackfoot people had changed beyond recognition. They had been a prosperous and independent nation at the time of the treaty, feared and respected from horizon to horizon. Now, they were ragged, hungry and poverty-stricken, their numbers sadly reduced and depending on the bounty of the government for survival. More than 1,000 of the Confederacy had died during the four years. The survivors were bewildered. They could not understand how their fortunes had changed so drastically in such a short time.

Crowfoot was saddened, but not bewildered. He had known that change was coming, although he had not expected it to come so soon. Crowfoot was even able to derive some

Blackfoot receiving rations

pleasure from the governor general's visit. Poundmaker was acting as interpreter on the tour. It did Crowfoot's heart good to meet his adopted son again.

In spite of the Blackfoot's appalling poverty, Crowfoot received the governor general with dignity, and made a frank and moving speech, in which he described the Blackfoot's desperate condition, asking that the rations be increased. Lord Lorne replied by suggesting that the Blackfoot should take up farming. Crowfoot agreed to try. But the lack of rations was the immediate problem.

Rations were half a kilogram of beef a day and a quarter-kilogram of flour per person. And this was not always received, for the food was not being distributed fairly. Offal and steers' heads were sold to the highest bidder instead of being handed out free. Women who turned to prostitution were given extra supplies. Occasionally, some families received nothing at all. And the flour was very often of such poor quality that it was not fit for human consumption.

The Blackfoot reserve was administered by civilian employees of the Indian Department, some of whom were rough, unimaginative people, with little or no experience of Aboriginal customs. These people spoke insultingly to the chiefs, making no attempt to hide the fact that they despised the Blackfoot. They had power and they abused it.

This put Crowfoot in a very awkward position. As a chief, it was his duty to see that his people were provided for and well treated. He complained to the authorities. He appealed to the Indian Agent; he attempted to negotiate for better conditions with the farm instructor, the senior government employee on the reserve. But these officials simply said he was a trouble-maker.

In fact, Crowfoot was working hard to prevent trouble. His warriors would willingly have attacked the hated government employees. It took all of Crowfoot's leadership skills to prevent them from doing so. The young men yielded to his authority, but they resented his policy, considering it weak and cowardly. Crowfoot was criticized on all sides even as he worked to make the best of impossible circumstances.

Things came to a head in 1882, when a dispute broke out between some government employees and a minor Blackfoot chief called Bull Elk. Bull Elk had bought a steer's head for a dollar, and one of the officials had taken it back, claiming there was too much meat on it. During the ensuing quarrel, Bull Elk fired off a couple of shots towards the ration house - and was promptly arrested by the Mounted Police. The Blackfoot were outraged. They had been seething with resentment for months. Now they turned on the police and tried to free Bull Elk. It looked as if there would be a pitched battle.

Cecil Denny is seen in the picture on page 47; (middle row, far left). In the front row are two Bloods, Elk Facing the Wind (left) and Black Eagle (right). The hatless man in the back row is Jerry Potts. Potts, half Piegan and half Scottish, was great help to the NWMP, both as guide and interpreter.

Frantically, the inspector of police sent a message to Crowfoot, hoping that he would be able to pacify the combatants. Crowfoot was just as angry as his people. Bull Elk declared that he was innocent. The police had no right to arrest him. Crowfoot allowed the police to take Bull Elk away only on condition that he would be able to attend the chief's trial. And, although at the trial Colonel Macleod agreed that there was no real case against the Blackfoot chief, he sentenced Bull Elk to fourteen days in the guardhouse for using a weapon in a threatening manner. This sentence did not please

Edgar Dewdney

Crowfoot or his people.

Fortunately, Edgar Dewdney, now lieutenant-governor of the North-West Territories as well as Indian Commissioner, had become aware of the discontent on the reserve. Like Macleod, he was a man of conscience - and also a shrewd administrator. Dewdney quickly removed the unpopular farm instructor from the reserve, replacing him with a former policeman known and liked by the Blackfoot. Dewdney also recalled the Indian Agent and gave the job to Cecil Denny.

This was a wise move. Denny had been an inspector in the Mounted Police, and was a long-standing friend of Crowfoot. He understood the Blackfoot people's predicament and sympathized with their complaints. As soon as he became Indian Agent, he began to set matters right, not only on Crowfoot's reserve, but on all those other resources affected by Treaty Number Seven. Denny made sure rations were distributed fairly and that the sale of offal and steers' heads was forbidden. He attended to less urgent problems, supplying wood for building, and making a determined effort to encourage farming. By the following year, Denny was able to report that "the Blackfeet, Bloods, and Piegans turned in one thousand, one hundred sacks of potatoes to be stored for their use in the agency root house."

Crowfoot's patience and pacifism had paid off, to the benefit of the tribe. Yet Crowfoot was uneasy about the future. Events of the past few years made him cynical. No longer did he believe the Mounted Police to be impartial. He had seen them side against the Blackfoot on more than one occasion, almost by instinct. Nor did he trust the government. Too many of its employees had proved to be untrustworthy. But Crowfoot still believed in the good faith of some individual white men. He appreciated the efforts of Cecil Denny and Lieutenant-Governor Dewdney. He thought highly of Father Lacombe and several other missionaries. Most important of all, he still had great faith in the honesty and integrity of Colonel Macleod.

Chapter 7
Rebellion or Neutrality

olonel Macleod was a rock of dependability during the difficult years when Crowfoot and his people were adjusting to their new way of life. Macleod was ideally suited to the difficult task of bringing peace and justice to the plains, for he had experience as a lawyer and as a soldier. He had practised law in Ontario before volunteering for the Mounted Police. He had also served in the militia, rising to the rank of lieutenant-colonel and receiving a C.M.G. for his part in the Red River expedition of 1870. Macleod was one of the first 300 men to volunteer for the North-West Mounted Police; he was appointed assistant commissioner within less than a year of joining the Force. In 1876, he was promoted to commissioner.

Lieutenant-Colonel James F. Macleod in uniform. James Farquharson Macleod was born on the Isle of Skye, Scotland, in 1836, and came to Canada with his family as a child. He was educated at Upper Canada College and Queen's University. He was assistant commissioner of NWMP 1874-75, and commissioner (in command of the entire force) 1876-80. He was appointed magistrate, and in 1887, he was made puisne judge of the Supreme Court of the North-West Territories. Macleod died four years after Crowfoot.

Macleod's personal qualities made him highly suitable for his job. It was said that he had "a manner which put strangers at their ease at once, but effectually prevented any undue familiarity." He was a good officer, seeing to the welfare of his men before looking after his own comforts. Equally important was his sincere concern for Aboriginal peoples. Macleod insisted the police be friendly and helpful to all Aboriginals and that they always act with rigid fairness. Macleod not only sought to establish law and order in the West; he wanted to gain the support and trust of the many Aboriginals who lived there.

Macleod had studied law, and he was interested in Blackfoot law; he carefully took it into account whenever an Aboriginal was on trial. Often he consulted with Crowfoot or one of the other chiefs so he could impose a suitable sentence, but one that would not be thought too harsh. And there were many occasions when he dismissed a case because the evidence

A horse-stealing expedition

was not strong enough. Macleod gained such a reputation for scrupulous fairness that the Blackfoot would allow a mere handful of police to come into their camps to make an arrest: they knew that the suspect would be released if he was innocent.

Most of Macleod's cases concerned settlers rather than Blackfoot. Aboriginal crime was confined almost entirely to horse-stealing – a long-standing tradition that died hard. In the past, a man gained great prestige when he raided an enemy camp and came away with the horses. Such raids were now forbidden, and chiefs like Crowfoot strived to prevent them. It was not easy. Horse-raiding was the only way young men thought they could prove their courage, now that honours through warfare were no longer possible. Macleod understood this. And, even though he prosecuted horse thieves firmly, he was lenient at first - provided the offenders were Aboriginal. Settlers and traders were treated more severely for they had no tradition to excuse their crime.

Macleod retired from the North-West Mounted Police in 1880, although he continued to serve in the West, as a magistrate and then as a judge. Thus he was a permanent influence at a time when everything else seemed to be falling apart. Crowfoot could look to Macleod for justice in the belief that the Blackfoot would be given a fair deal. And he could continue to hope that his people would gain most by cooperating with the Canadian government.

Cecil Edward Denny was another person who helped Crowfoot maintain his faith during these years. Denny was the man who was made Indian Agent for the Treaty Number Seven tribes in 1882. He was a difficult character who did not always get on with his superiors, but he was also very popular with the First Nations. In 1879, as a NWMP inspector at Fort Calgary (which he had named), Denny took it upon himself to buy meat for Crowfoot's band and for the many others who had hunted in vain for buffalo. Typically, Denny did not wait to get permission to spend government money. He saw the Blackfoot in desperate straits and took immediate action.

Like Macleod, Denny was one of the original 300 to volunteer for the Mounted Police, and he knew the Blackfoot well. Once he settled a murder case according to Native law, rather than "Queen's Law:" one of Crowfoot's band had killed a Cree; Denny arranged a council meeting between Crowfoot and the Cree chiefs. Crowfoot was eager to find a peaceful solution, even though he felt it was the Cree who had initiated the trouble. Crowfoot agreed to smoke with Denny and the opposing chiefs, and between them they settled the affair traditionally: the Blackfoot would pay a number of horses to the family of the slain man, provided the Cree band would leave the area.

Denny understood and admired the Blackfoot, and he was the right man to take the job as Indian Agent in 1882 when there was trouble on the reserve. But Denny resigned after only two years. In 1884, the deputy superintendent general of Indian Affairs in Ottawa issued a series of instructions which Denny in all conscience could not follow. Among other things, he was ordered to cut rations and told he could visit each reserve no more than once a month. Another order forbidding the Blackfoot to leave their reserves was also issued.

A few years earlier, the Canadian government had instituted a policy which required all Aboriginals to obtain permits when they wanted to travel outside their reserves. Now, these permits were refused, contrary to Treaty #7, which clearly stated that First Nations would be allowed to move freely throughout the territory. Yet there was good reason for

Denny reported later to Colonel Macleod: They are actually dying of starvation (I have already heard of 21 cases of death). As they are and have been getting no assistance from any post, I took upon myself the responsibility of purchasing and issuing beef to them. For the last three days I have been obliged to issue beef at the rate of 2,000 pounds per diem. The Blackfeet are utterly destitute, there being no buffalo in the country. I have had to send out meat to parties on their way in, who are eating grass to keep themselves alive.

Metis leader Louis Riel

the government order; in 1884 Louis Riel was mustering support among Canada's Aboriginal people. They would be less likely to rise in a body if they were isolated in their separate reserves.

The restrictions in travel added fuel to the smouldering fire, and the Blackfoot became even more distrustful of government. Rations had been cut drastically since Denny's departure - and they might even be cut back further on the order of some official in faraway Ottawa. Even Crowfoot began to listen to talk of rebellion.

In spite of the efforts of the Mounted Police, Riel's messengers roamed the country, visiting First Nations and urging them to rise against the government. One of the messengers, a Metis called Bear's Head, managed to visit the Blackfoot camp during the Sun Dance in 1884. Bear's Head had already been imprisoned for vagrancy. He was arrested again by the police while actually sitting beside Crowfoot in Crowfoot's lodge. This time the charge was "disturbing the peace."

Crowfoot was furiously angry, and very nearly disturbed the peace himself in his efforts to stop the Mounties from taking Bear's Head away. Crowfoot could not see that the man had done anything wrong - and indeed Bear's Head was acquitted when brought to trial, but he was ordered to leave the district. Crowfoot felt this ruling was extremely unjust. He felt the police had victimized Bear's Head.

Crowfoot began to consider Louis Riel's cause seriously. He had come to know Riel quite well during the years the Blackfoot had been in Montana. In those days Crowfoot had seen no reason to support the Metis cause: the Mounted Police were his friends, and he trusted the Dominion government. Now circumstances had changed. Crowfoot no longer had much faith in the police or the government. Those in authority did not seem to care. The Blackfoot had been humiliated by the behaviour of petty officials too often.

Perhaps they might at least gain control of their own destiny if they rose in rebellion.

Crowfoot knew he had only to say the word. His people were eager for battle. They had had enough. Then, Lieutenant-Governor Dewdney intervened personally.

Winnipeg, 1885.
Winnipeg had a population of about 15,000 in 1884.

He was worried by the unrest on the Confederacy reserves, and he invited Crowfoot and the other leading chiefs to visit Winnipeg and Regina. This was a very clever move because, in these fast-growing cities, the chiefs were able to see how many thousands of people had settled in the West already. "They are as plentiful as flies in the summertime," Crowfoot would say later. "It is useless to oppose them."

When the Northwest Rebellion broke out in the spring of 1885, Crowfoot held his hand, watching to see how things would develop before committing his people to warfare. He sent messengers to Red Crow at the Blood reserve and to Eagle Tail, head chief of the Piegans, asking if they intended to support the rebels. Both replied that they did not. These men had also visited Winnipeg and Regina, and in any case, conditions were improving on the reserves. Dewdney persuaded Cecil Denny to resume the job of Indian Agent, authorizing him to act "in any way which you may deem advisable." Denny deemed it advisable to increase rations, and he doubled them immediately, removing one major anxiety.

Nevertheless, Crowfoot remained undecided. He was a practised diplomat with long years of decision-making behind him, and he would not be taken in by last-minute efforts at

Crowfoot with a rifle

appeasement. And, his sympathies were with the rebels. Poundmaker, his adopted son, had been caught up in the troubles, and Crowfoot longed to go to his aid. He knew he could count on the support of his soldiers, and that other people from the Confederacy would surely follow if he chose to fight.

But Crowfoot's dilemma was this. Although he would willingly have sacrificed his own life for Poundmaker, he did not want the Confederacy to suffer. And Crowfoot suspected that the Confederacy would indeed suffer. He knew the government's strength. He knew that the recently built railway, which ran past the Blackfoot reserve, could bring thousands of troops from the east in an amazingly short time. He also knew that the Blackfoot depended on the government for food. So, even if the rising was successful, his people might well face starvation.

There was another problem. The Cree and Metis were counting on Blackfoot support. The Cree had threatened to take vengeance if the Blackfoot did not join the rebellion. Although Crowfoot was not a man who could be influenced by threats, he was gravely concerned for the safety of his people.

Crowfoot was still pondering his strategy when Lieutenant-Governor Dewdney came to see him. Dewdney was worried. There were wild rumours that the Blackfoot were planning to attack Calgary. Father Lacombe had visited the reserve and reported that all was quiet there, but Dewdney was not entirely satisfied. He wanted to visit the reserve himself in an effort to win the Blackfoot round.

The lieutenant-governor and Crowfoot had a long frank talk. Dewdney promised Crowfoot that neither the rebels nor the army would be allowed to molest the Blackfoot in any way. He assured Crowfoot the Blackfoot could count on government protection, not only in the present crisis, but also in the future. In fact, he made it clear that the Blackfoot had everything to gain by remaining peaceable.

Crowfoot trusted Dewdney. Time and again, the

At right: Telegram from Father Lacombe to the prime minister

Rebellion or Neutrality

Copy

Form 167.

Canadian Pacific Railway Co
WESTERN DIVISION.

24 Collect

The following message received at _____ C _____ Time 845P M.

By Telegraph from _____ Blackfoot Crossing

Date _____ 30th _____ 188 5

To _____ Sir John MacDonald

Ottawa

I have seen Crowfoot
& all the Blackfeet all
quiet promised me to
be loyal no matter
how the things may
turn Elsewhere

Father Lacombe

lieutenant-governor had shown his concern for First Nations. He was a man of his word and, equally importantly, a man with the authority to see that promises were kept.

After his meeting with Dewdney was finished, Crowfoot sent a message to Sir John A. Macdonald, assuring the prime minister that the Blackfoot would remain loyal to the Queen. This message was received with relief in Ottawa – as Crowfoot knew it would be. He was a very astute politician. By declaring his loyalty so publicly, he automatically gave the Blackfoot a measure of protection by removing suspicion from them.

One of Crowfoot's most famous sayings was "Makakit ki Eyekakimat" (Be wise and persevere).

Crowfoot's followers were not at all pleased by his announcement. They had expected him to fight, and felt he was being cowardly. Crowfoot was 55 years old and by this time there was a generation gap between him and the younger men of his band, who had not known their chief during his warrior years. They saw only a tired, elderly leader, who seemed too eager to take the cautious path of appeasement. They wanted glory, not conciliation. But Crowfoot was not to be influenced by their criticism. He had the moral strength to put his people's welfare before his own popularity.

So the Blackfoot remained quietly on the reserve throughout the rebellion, though many of Crowfoot's followers despised him for their inaction. Crowfoot's sympathies were with the rebels. He sympathized openly, giving shelter to any Cree refugees who came to his camp. This caused many neighbouring settlers to suspect his loyalty. They did not understand that Crowfoot's first loyalties were to the First Nations peoples - not to Queen Victoria or Sir John A. Macdonald.

Perhaps in the long run, Crowfoot might have taken up arms if the rising had had some hope of success. Nobody will ever know how close he came to open rebellion in 1885. But some credit for his neutrality must go to Edgar Dewdney, Cecil Denny and James Macleod. Crowfoot had known these men for a good many years. They had never let him down. Without the long-standing record of friendship and trustworthiness, Crowfoot might well have felt his people would have nothing to lose by opposing the government. But as it was, he kept the peace, to the benefit of the Blackfoot - and ultimately the entire nation.

56   Rebellion or Neutrality

Chapter 8
A Peacemaker to the End

When the Northwest Rebellion ended in June, Crowfoot regained much of his lost prestige. He had protected his people wisely and most of them were prepared to admit it. His reputation was high in other circles too. He was hailed as a hero in the East – a loyal chief who had prevented the Confederacy from taking up arms.

But Crowfoot was not jubilant. Poundmaker, his prized adopted son, was in prison, charged with rebellion. Poundmaker wrote to Crowfoot, as did the Lieutenant-Governor, and he was slightly cheered when he received a reply. He was also comforted to hear from Dewdney, who promised to visit Poundmaker to make sure he was being well treated. Dewdney worked hard for the prisoner's release. This was partly to appease Crowfoot and partly because Poundmaker was not well. Trouble might well break out afresh should Poundmaker die in prison.

In March 1886, Poundmaker was set free; he paid Crowfoot a visit a few weeks later. This made the old chief happier than he had been for a long time. But it was not to last. Poundmaker was very ill, and died in July while celebrating the Sun Dance with his adopted father.

Crowfoot was distraught. All his children seemed to be dying. Now his beloved adopted son was gone as well. A newspaper report of 1925 stated that Crowfoot had no children of his own. This report blandly ignores one of the major tragedies of Crowfoot's life, for he had a great many children, nearly all of whom succumbed to tuberculosis, one after the other in 1885 and 1886, while Crowfoot looked on helplessly, unable to help.

It was while in mourning for Poundmaker and the dead youngsters that Crowfoot met Sir John A. Macdonald for the first time. The prime minister visited the Blackfoot reserve in

Poundmaker had been drawn into the rebellion unwillingly, and he had actually prevented the Cree from massacring the army at Cut Knife Hill. "I saved a lot of bloodshed," he said at his trial. "I can't understand how it is that after saving many lives I am brought here."

Crowfoot with his children in 1884

the course of his opening journey across Canada on the Canadian Pacific Railway. Some years earlier, Crowfoot had given permission for the railway to run its track alongside the reserve; he had been told that it would help the Blackfoot by bringing them regular food supplies. In fact the railroad brought nothing but trouble. Sparks from the trains caused fires. Horses were run over on the tracks. More and more settlers poured into the district. And there was a suspicion that the sickness which was sweeping the reserve came from the smoke of the railway engines.

Nevertheless, Crowfoot received the prime minister graciously, and the two men got on well together. Genial as always, Macdonald invited Crowfoot to come to Ottawa later in the year, and the chief accepted.

The visit to Ottawa developed into a grand tour during which Crowfoot was taken through several eastern Canadian cities. In Montreal he met William Van Horne, who presented him with a free lifetime pass for the Canadian Pacific Railway. In Ottawa he visited the Macdonalds at their residence. Everywhere there were speeches and receptions and state functions. Crowfoot's stepbrother, Three Bulls, and Red Crow of the Blood tribe also took part in the tour, as did several other "loyal chiefs," accompanied by Father Lacombe and interpreter Jean L'Heureux. Crowfoot, however, was the star. His name was a household word, and everyone wanted to meet him.

While the citizens of the East were gazing in wonder at the chiefs of the West, the chiefs themselves were looking around and taking everything in. Crowfoot was satisfied he had acted for the best during the rebellion. He could see that his Blackfoot warriors could not possibly have won. He also had proof that there were many other people as well-intentioned as Macleod and Dewdney. Crowfoot was pleased to be able to demonstrate his gratitude to Dewdney that same winter, for the lieutenant-governor was in danger of losing his job. When Crowfoot returned to his reserve, he prepared a petition supporting Dewdney.

Crowfoot was far from well when he returned home. His eastern tour had to be cut short because of illness. Crowfoot became weaker as the months passed. But he maintained his influence in the Confederacy. In 1887, he visited the Blood reserve, and helped Red Crow prevent some Blood warriors

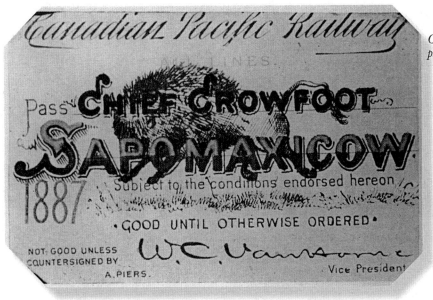

Crowfoot's railway pass

Crowfoot in Ottawa with Father Lacombe and Three Bulls

A Peacemaker to the End

Further Reading

Barnett, Donald C. *Poundmaker*, Toronto: Fitzhenry & Whiteside, 1976.

Dempsey, Hugh A. *Crowfoot: Chief of the Blackfeet*, Edmonton: Hurtig, 1972.

Dickason, Olive. *Canada's First Nations*, Toronto: Oxford, 1997.

Ewers, John C. *The Blackfeet: Raiders of the Northwestern Plains*. Oklahoma: University of Oklahoma Press, 1958 (1993).

McGhee, Robert. *Ancient Canada*, Ottawa: Canadian Museum of Civilization, 1989.

Morris, Alexander, *The Treaties of Canada with the Indians of Manitoba and the North-West Territories, Including the Negotiations on Which They Were Based, and Other Information Relating Thereto*, Toronto: Willing and Williamson, 1880 (Facsimile reprint, Calgary, Fifth House).

Neering, Rosemary, *Louis Riel*. Toronto: Fitzhenry & Whiteside, 1977, 1999.

Neering, Rosemary, *Settlement of the West*, Toronto: Fitzhenry & Whiteside, 1974.

Ewers, John C. *The Blackfeet: Their art and culture:* Hancock House, 1987

Lindeman, Frank B. *Blackfeet Indians*, Crown, 1995

Credits

The author is most grateful to the staff of the Glenbow-Alberta Institute and to Mr. S.W. Horrall, Historian to the Royal Canadian Mounted Police, for their kind assistance.

The author and publishers wish to express their gratitude to J.M.Dent and Sons (Canada) Ltd. for permission to quote from *The Law Marches West* by Sir Cecil E. Denny; and to the following:

Canada Post, page 34
Canadian Pacific, page 59
Glenbow-Alberta Institute, pages 3, 7, 11, 14, 19, 22, 26, 27, 29, 31, 39, 42, 45, 47, 48, 49, 50, 54, 55, 58, 60, 61, 62
Richard Gregory, pages 5, 40
Provincial Archives of Alberta, pages 6, 9, 20, 24, 27, 52, 53
Public Archives of Canada, pages 28, 33
Royal Canadian Mounted Police, page 17
Every effort has been made to credit all sources correctly. The author and publishers will welcome information that would allow them to correct any errors or omissions.

Crowfoot, late in life

from going off to raid the Gros Ventre in Montana. During the last year of his life, Crowfoot paid several visits to other reserves in an effort to promote peace and a sense of brotherhood among the First Nations.

On his own reserve, he did his best to encourage his people to adapt to their new way of life. Farming would have to replace hunting if the Blackfoot were to prosper, and Crowfoot set an example by hoeing his own land. But, though his spirit was as strong as ever, his strength was failing. Crowfoot began to cough blood, as so many of his children had done. He knew that his time was running out.

Crowfoot died at Blackfoot Crossing on 25 April, 1890. He maintained his role as peacemaker right to the end. As he lay dying in his tipi – dressed in full regalia and surrounded by friends and relatives – Crowfoot delivered a message to his people urging them to remain on good terms with their neighbours, the settlers. He thanked the government for its aid to the Blackfoot; he thanked the government doctor who had ministered to him in his illness; he sent a message of thanks to Dewdney. And, like a true Blackfoot, he faced death without fear. He was eloquent, as always:

A little while and Crowfoot will be gone from among you; whither we cannot tell. From nowhere we come, into nowhere we go. What is life? It is as the flash of a firefly in the night. It is a breath of a buffalo in the winter time. It is as the little shadow that runs across the grass and loses itself in the sunset. I have spoken.

It was not only the Blackfoot who mourned in the weeks that followed Crowfoot's death. Macleod, Dewdney and many others felt a deep sense of personal loss. Canadians across the country paid tribute to the great chief.

Predictably, the tributes praised Crowfoot's loyalty more often than his statesmanship. Yet he was a great statesman and politician. Only a highly skilled diplomat could have led his people so astutely through the series of calamities which had befallen them. Whether making long-reaching decisions or settling minor grievances, Crowfoot had unerringly taken the right course at the right time.

Even his disastrous journey to Montana had been sensible in the circumstances - most of his people would have gone anyway. The Blackfoot would never have agreed to settle on a reserve while there were still buffalo herds in the south. The band would have been divided and, inevitably, many Blackfoot would have been killed. The young men would have fared poorly in Montana without Crowfoot's moderating influence.

But Crowfoot's wisest decision was surely to remain neutral during the Northwest Rebellion. The most appalling slaughter might have occurred had his people gone to war. As it was, the Blackfoot were unmolested and, for a time at least, favoured. The people survived and struggled on, in spite of successive missionaries

who - in all good faith - tried to "cleanse" them of their culture; and they survived in spite of unimaginative Indian Agents who stopped their rations in an effort to force them into farming. In later years, the Blackfoot would often suffer discrimination and injustice, but at least Crowfoot had assured them of survival. He had seen his people safely through their great transition.

Born to be a warrior, destined to become a peacemaker, Crowfoot threaded his way adeptly through a maze of complicated problems by constantly remaining true to his people and true to his principles. He stood for courage, loyalty, patience, honesty, generosity - virtues that are as old as humankind.

His life was gentle, and the elements
So mix'd in him that Nature might stand up
And say to all the world, "This was a man!"
(William Shakespeare)

from going off to raid the Gros Ventre in Montana. During the last year of his life, Crowfoot paid several visits to other reserves in an effort to promote peace and a sense of brotherhood among the First Nations.

Crowfoot, late in life

On his own reserve, he did his best to encourage his people to adapt to their new way of life. Farming would have to replace hunting if the Blackfoot were to prosper, and Crowfoot set an example by hoeing his own land. But, though his spirit was as strong as ever, his strength was failing. Crowfoot began to cough blood, as so many of his children had done. He knew that his time was running out.

Crowfoot died at Blackfoot Crossing on 25 April, 1890. He maintained his role as peacemaker right to the end. As he lay dying in his tipi – dressed in full regalia and surrounded by friends and relatives – Crowfoot delivered a message to his people urging them to remain on good terms with their neighbours, the settlers. He thanked the government for its aid to the Blackfoot; he thanked the government doctor who had ministered to him in his illness; he sent a message of thanks to Dewdney. And, like a true Blackfoot, he faced death without fear. He was eloquent, as always:

A little while and Crowfoot will be gone from among you; whither we cannot tell. From nowhere we come, into nowhere we go. What is life? It is as the flash of a firefly in the night. It is a breath of a buffalo in the winter time. It is as the little shadow that runs across the grass and loses itself in the sunset. I have spoken.

It was not only the Blackfoot who mourned in the weeks that followed Crowfoot's death. Macleod, Dewdney and many others felt a deep sense of personal loss. Canadians across the country paid tribute to the great chief.

Predictably, the tributes praised Crowfoot's loyalty more often than his statesmanship. Yet he was a great statesman and politician. Only a highly skilled diplomat could have led his people so astutely through the series of calamities which had befallen them. Whether making long-reaching decisions or settling minor grievances, Crowfoot had unerringly taken the right course at the right time.

Even his disastrous journey to Montana had been sensible in the circumstances - most of his people would have gone anyway. The Blackfoot would never have agreed to settle on a reserve while there were still buffalo herds in the south. The band would have been divided and, inevitably, many Blackfoot would have been killed. The young men would have fared poorly in Montana without Crowfoot's moderating influence.

But Crowfoot's wisest decision was surely to remain neutral during the Northwest Rebellion. The most appalling slaughter might have occurred had his people gone to war. As it was, the Blackfoot were unmolested and, for a time at least, favoured. The people survived and struggled on, in spite of successive missionaries

who - in all good faith - tried to "cleanse" them of their culture; and they survived in spite of unimaginative Indian Agents who stopped their rations in an effort to force them into farming. In later years, the Blackfoot would often suffer discrimination and injustice, but at least Crowfoot had assured them of survival. He had seen his people safely through their great transition.

Born to be a warrior, destined to become a peacemaker, Crowfoot threaded his way adeptly through a maze of complicated problems by constantly remaining true to his people and true to his principles. He stood for courage, loyalty, patience, honesty, generosity - virtues that are as old as humankind.

His life was gentle, and the elements
So mix'd in him that Nature might stand up
And say to all the world, "This was a man!"
(William Shakespeare)

Further Reading

Barnett, Donald C. *Poundmaker,* Toronto: Fitzhenry & Whiteside, 1976.

Dempsey, Hugh A. *Crowfoot: Chief of the Blackfeet,* Edmonton: Hurtig, 1972

Dickason, Olive. *Canada's First Nations,* Toronto: Oxford, 1997.

Ewers, John C. *The Blackfeet: Raiders of the Northwestern Plains.* Oklahoma: University of Oklahoma Press, 1958 (1993).

McGhee, Robert. *Ancient Canada,* Ottawa: Canadian Museum of Civilization, 1989.

Morris, Alexander, *The Treaties of Canada with the Indians of Manitoba and the North-West Territories, Including the Negotiations on Which They Were Based, and Other Information Relating Thereto,* Toronto: Willing and Williamson, 1880 (Facsimile reprint, Calgary, Fifth House).

Neering, Rosemary, *Louis Riel.* Toronto: Fitzhenry & Whiteside, 1977, 1999.

Neering, Rosemary, *Settlement of the West,* Toronto: Fitzhenry & Whiteside, 1974.

Ewers, John C. *The Blackfeet: Their art and culture:* Hancock House, 1987

Lindeman, Frank B. *Blackfeet Indians,* Crown, 1995

Credits

The author is most grateful to the staff of the Glenbow-Alberta Institute and to Mr. S.W. Horrall, Historian to the Royal Canadian Mounted Police, for their kind assistance.

The author and publishers wish to express their gratitude to J.M.Dent and Sons (Canada) Ltd. for permission to quote from *The Law Marches West* by Sir Cecil E. Denny; and to the following:
Canada Post, page 34
Canadian Pacific, page 59
Glenbow-Alberta Institute, pages 3, 7, 11, 14, 19, 22, 26, 27, 29, 31, 39, 42, 45, 47, 48, 49, 50, 54, 55, 58, 60, 61, 62
Richard Gregory, pages 5, 40
Provincial Archives of Alberta, pages 6, 9, 20, 24, 37, 52, 53
Public Archives of Canada, pages 28, 33
Royal Canadian Mounted Police, page 17
Every effort has been made to credit all sources correctly. The author and publishers will welcome information that would allow them to correct any errors or omissions.

Index